BOOK OF NO LEDGE

BOOK OF NO LEDGE

NANCE VAN WINCKEL

Nance Van Winckel

ISBN: 978-0-8071-6540-9

Published by Pleiades Press

Department of English
University of Central Missouri
Warrensbsurg, Missouri 64093

Distributed by Louisiana State University Press

Cover design and layout by David Wojciechowski
Author's photo by Patricia Henley

First Pleiades Printing, 2016

Financial Assistance for this project has been provided by the Missouri Arts Council,
a state agency, and the National Endowment for the Arts.

CONTENTS

BOOK OF NO LEDGE

As usual it starts with love. I had my heart set on the door-to-door encyclopedia sales boy. Maybe 18 or 19, he said he was working his way through college. He winked a turquoise eye at me and asked if I was the "lady of the house."

Well, I wasn't. I was 13-going-on-17 and vaguely trying to flirt. After my mother came out on the porch and said NO, we don't need any books, I followed him down the walk and told him to come back tomorrow after I'd had a chance to "work on" her. Sure, he shrugged, why not.

When the cute guy returned the next day, he was all business. I watched as he showed my parents the full set. The pages were silky. Thirteen volumes and an index. As I passed Volume N (with the information about how the nose worked!) back to him, he gave me an appreciative nod. My tween-size heart felt too large for my chest. It was my dad who was all for the purchase, his family being a bit more "bookish" than my mother's.

Of course once the check was written, the boy evaporated into summer's mist, never to be seen again. But I could walk by and caress the books and in so doing call him into my mind, which I did for years. For years I dipped into those encyclopedias. The knowledge of the world was inside. I perused. I skimmed. With friendly and helpful manners and

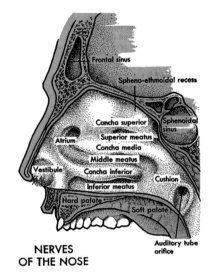

NERVES OF THE NOSE

the smoothest, most confident voice of The World, an all-knowing authority, almost god-like, spoke from the text. Dinosaurs. The sad and short lives of writers I was just beginning to read. The ALL I needed to know about the many states in which my family would live.

Every page offered a surprise! Every page featured Mr. Explainer giving me the lowdown with a winking turquoise eye, a nod, or sometimes a shrug because I was getting older and the books had begun to have a bit of a musty smell and he was beginning to feel unsure I still loved him as I had, especially when I turned into a much older woman and had these nice sharp scissors and even X-acto blades, and Oh, you're not certain that the white man helped the tribal people as well as I've so carefully outlined? No, dear, the solar flares *aren't* scary. Please don't fret. And please point that glue stick elsewhere. Surely you won't chop away that whole paragraph about the wonderful westward expansion and put some little poem in its place. A poem is not a fact, dear. Wait! We've been together for almost half a century! How could you! You know I loved you first. You know I loved you best!

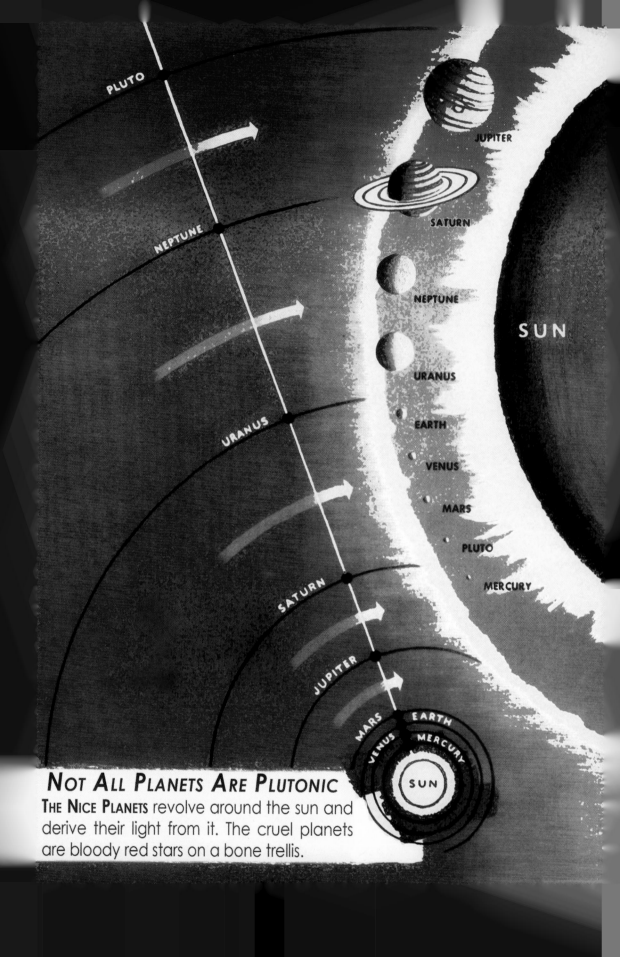

PLUTO

NEPTUNE

URANUS

SATURN

JUPITER

MARS

VENUS EARTH

MERCURY

SUN

JUPITER

SATURN

NEPTUNE

URANUS

EARTH

VENUS

MARS

PLUTO

MERCURY

SUN

NOT ALL PLANETS ARE PLUTONIC

THE NICE PLANETS revolve around the sun and derive their light from it. The cruel planets are bloody red stars on a bone trellis.

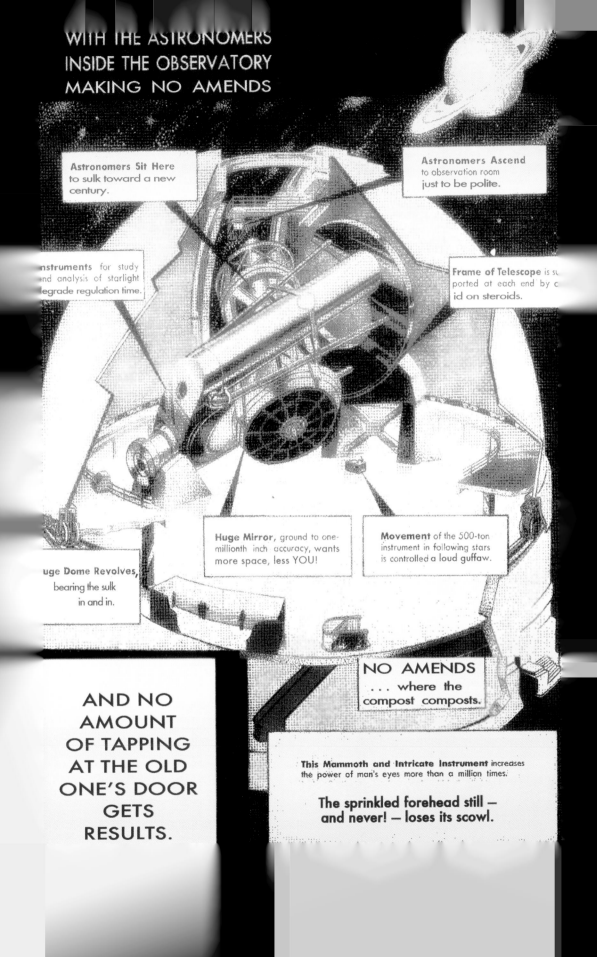

WITH THE ASTRONOMERS
INSIDE THE OBSERVATORY
MAKING NO AMENDS

Astronomers Sit Here to sulk toward a new century.

Astronomers Ascend to observation room just to be polite.

...nstruments for study ...nd analysis of starlight ...egrade regulation time.

Frame of Telescope is su... ...ported at each end by c... ...id on steroids.

Huge Mirror, ground to one-millionth inch accuracy, wants more space, less YOU!

Movement of the 500-ton instrument in following stars is controlled a loud guffaw.

...uge Dome Revolves, bearing the sulk in and in.

NO AMENDS
. . . where the compost composts.

AND NO AMOUNT OF TAPPING AT THE OLD ONE'S DOOR GETS RESULTS.

This Mammoth and Intricate Instrument increases the power of man's eyes more than a million times.

**The sprinkled forehead still —
and never! — loses its scowl.**

THE BRAIN PAN NEEDS ROOM FOR THE BRAIN!

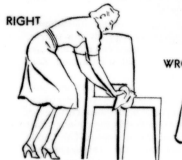

RIGHT

Out may fall meat on a mission!

WRONG

Around a curve the dream going too fast may drop its cargo.

Thin slices of brain on slides; then into the pan they go frying.

WRONG

RIGHT

Straight from the pan they're salty and sweet.

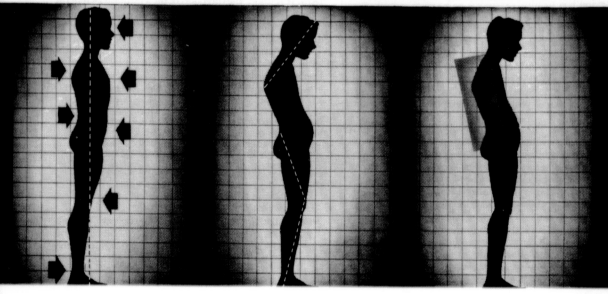

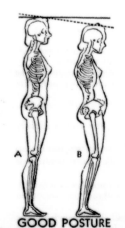

GOOD POSTURE

Correct posture, *left* (A), is ensured by holding the body in a balanced position; faulty posture makes a person seem shorter, *left* (B). To test posture, stand with back to wall as shown, *center*. Space at back of waist should be about thickness of the hand.

NECK
SPINE
PELVIC BONE CENTER OF WEIGHT
KNEES
LINE OF BALANCE

TRUNK

TESTING POSTURE

HOW TO RELAX

To stand at ease, *right*, place one foot slightly ahead of other; relax abdomen; keep chest high and shoulders back. To relax in a chair, *above*, sit well back. Place one foot forward on the floor and keep head as high as comfort will permit.

The Ex-Lover Arsonist

All Vortices

Basement Access

Horribilities

Morphs

Sorrow

EVERYONE NEEDS

POETRY INSURANCE

Shunned Poems

You wake in the wrong arms—someone who scratches in his sleep like a dog.

You must have married him when you wer too young to care.

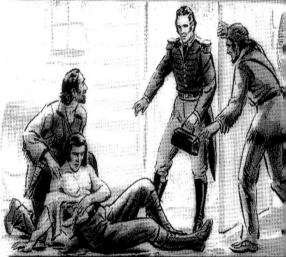

"Little fuckhead," you swore at your old face in the glass.

The fuckhead stared back, nonplussed, in your rage.

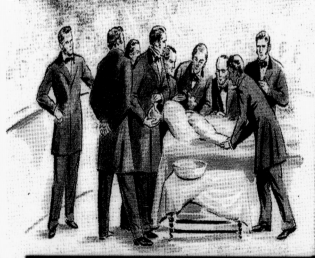

You did. You tried. Slept as hard and fast as you could but woke as an infant, quite unable—however Herculean the effort—to turn yourself over inside the crib's bright white bars.

Supports aircraft

Pushes sailboat

Used to pump water

Runs windmill

Supports parachute

Keeps patients alive in Iron Lung

Keeps water out of Caisson

Used for sandblasting buildings

Used for Welding

Runs motors

Defiling Even Air

All's already happened. Remote
mechanics. Blood out of (where?
what?) stones. Small acts (in alleys!
in cellars!) still steer our lives.
    Waking to the present
is a heavy jolt of *I*. A moment ago
you'd been Eve's head on a stake
staring across the ravaged garden.

Operates air hammer

Operates airbrush for painting

Carries sound

HOUSEHOLD USES

Inflates tires

Keeps ink in fountain pen

Electric fan

Creates musical tones

Picks up dust in vacuum cleaner

Keeps liquid in medicine dropper

Ventilation

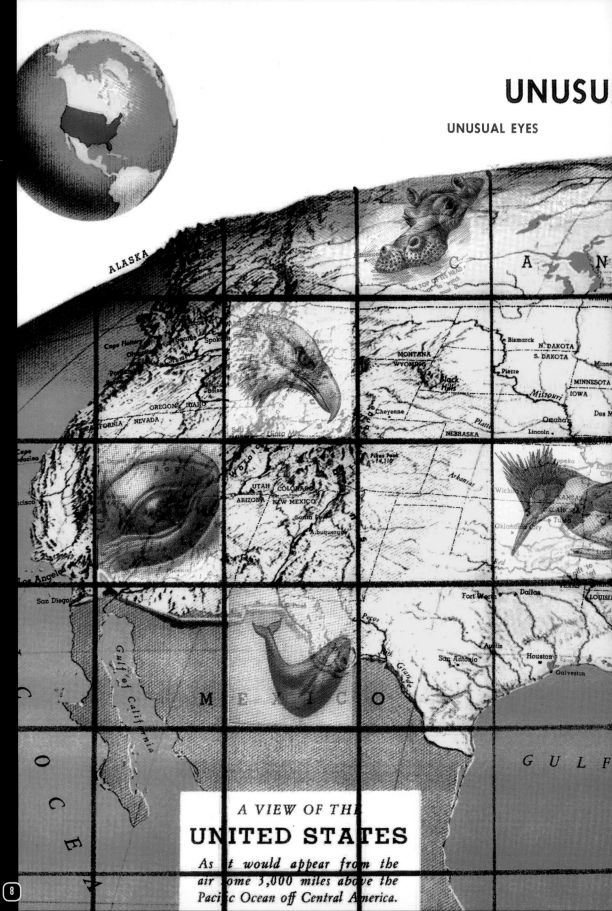

A VIEW OF THE
UNITED STATES
As it would appear from the
air some 3,000 miles above the
Pacific Ocean off Central America.

EYES

UNUSUAL EYES

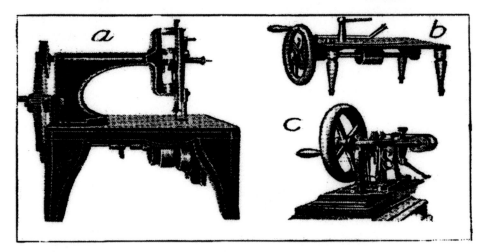

Early Sewing Machines. (a) The Singer; (b) Wilson's earliest model; (c) Elias Howe's original sewing machine

The Eyes! The Eyes Have All Had It.

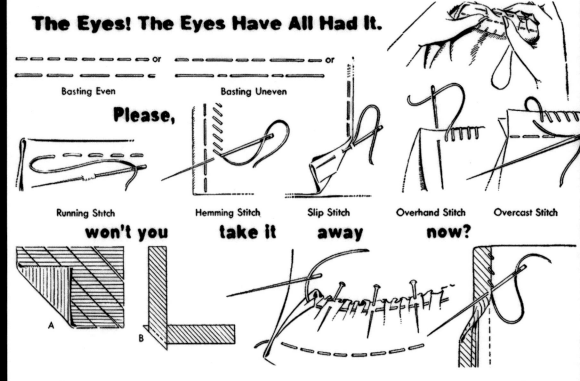

Basting Even   Basting Uneven

Please,

Running Stitch   Hemming Stitch   Slip Stitch   Overhand Stitch   Overcast Stitch

won't you   **take it**   **away**   **now?**

—That lap robe made from the horse you rode as a child.

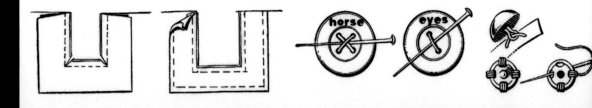

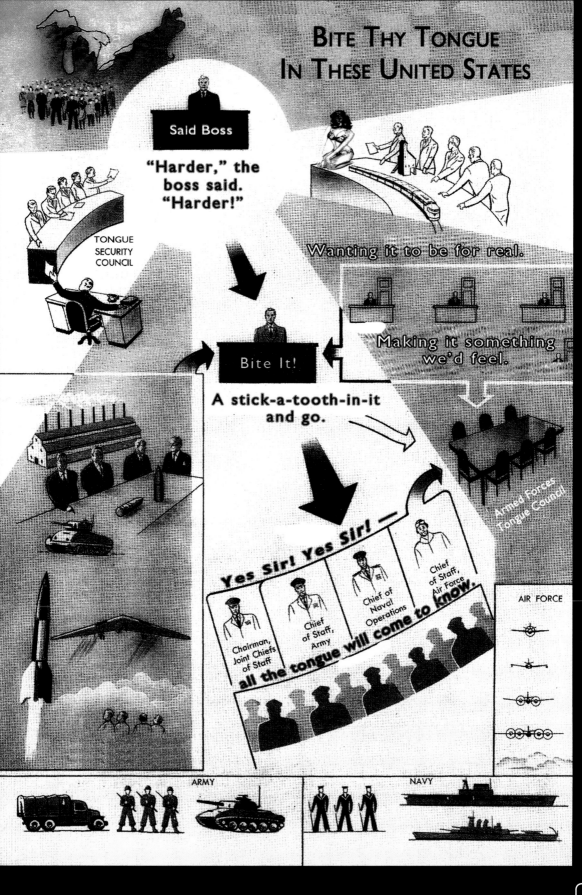

REVOKE OUR SYMBOLS

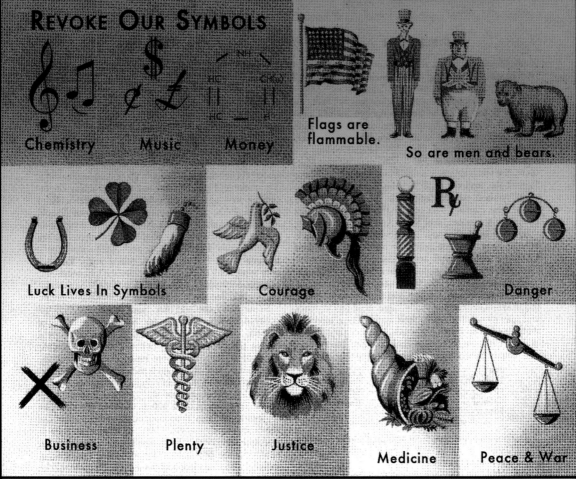

Chemistry   Music   Money

Flags are flammable.

So are men and bears.

Luck Lives In Symbols   Courage   Danger

Business   Plenty   Justice   Medicine   Peace & War

SYLVITE, *SIL vite.* See POTASH.

SYLVIUS, AENEAS. See PIUS (II).

SYMBIOSIS, *sim by O sis,* is the name given to the partnership of two different kinds of organisms, such as two plants or a plant and animal, in which both organisms benefit. Such a partnership occurs often in nature. For example, a fungus and an alga sometimes grow together and form a *lichen,* which is different from either plant. Each organism benefits from this close association. The fungus, which cannot produce its own food, gets its food from the alga. The alga gets protection from the fungus. See LICHEN.

SYMBOL. A symbol is a sign which stands for some object or an idea. All words are symbols. Spoken words are symbols for objects and ideas. The letters of the alphabet are symbols for certain sounds. These letters are combined to form the written words which are the symbols for spoken words.

One of the most familiar symbols of all nations is the national flag. To every person the flag of his nation means "my country." The military insignia worn on the uniform of a man in the armed services are symbols. They show to which service he belongs, what rank he holds, and what his duties are.

SYMBIOTICAL: what flesh of you
he dared not put his hands on
his breath whispered across,
though first he'd had to pass your
tea-drinking minions in the courtyard.

SYMBIOTICAL: Driving by the building
—disheveled in the new century— you
feel the bloat of a past tense.

SYMBOLICAL: The fingers' entrée.
The fingers' limits. A mouth's
boundaries. The drawn drapes,
the held breaths.

SYMBOLICAL: The shelf full of wide-
eyed bisque dolls watching.
The courtyard's teacups: white
leaves twittering on dead trees.

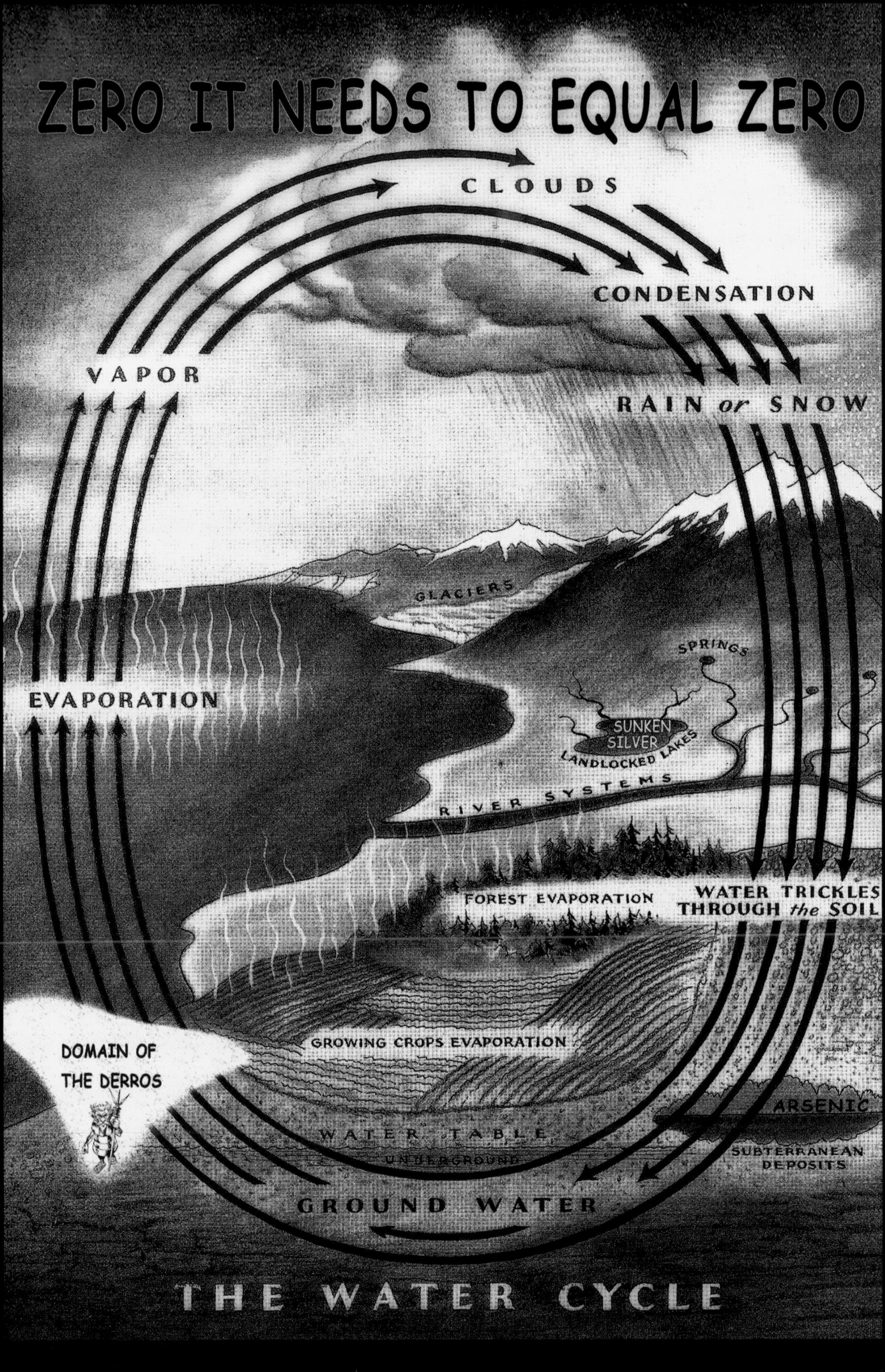

ZERO IT NEEDS TO EQUAL ZERO

CLOUDS

CONDENSATION

VAPOR

RAIN *or* SNOW

GLACIERS

SPRINGS

EVAPORATION

SUNKEN SILVER

LANDLOCKED LAKES

RIVER SYSTEMS

FOREST EVAPORATION

WATER TRICKLES THROUGH *the* SOIL

DOMAIN OF THE DERROS

GROWING CROPS EVAPORATION

ARSENIC

WATER TABLE UNDERGROUND

SUBTERRANEAN DEPOSITS

GROUND WATER

THE WATER CYCLE

1. Building a Cairn

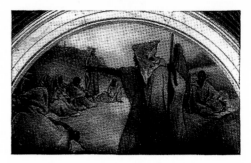

2. Storytelling

THE DEVELOPMENT OF THE BOOK

How to Use Books. Books serve many useful purposes. Some books, like *Tom Sawyer* or *The Wind in the Willows*, are read for pleasure and entertainment alone. Other books, for example, history books, give information about how people lived years ago and what they did and thought. Others, like the dictionary, answer questions as to how a word is spelled or what it means. Still others, like the atlas, show where cities and countries are located on the earth.

3. Egyptian Hieroglyphics

SAY *THIS*, AND SAY IT *THIS* WAY

The old one's tongue was trying to flap on in the young one's mouth. Words as curtsies. Hadn't she been a girl once? Hadn't she curled her hair with a poker hot from the fire? The smoke of her scorch settled on the mounting ringlets.

Avec plaisir, Madame. Just as instructed. And so they slipped from time together for a while, and all they wrought upon the world could be forgiven. Or so thought they.

4. Picture Writing

5. Copying Manuscripts

6. The Printing Press

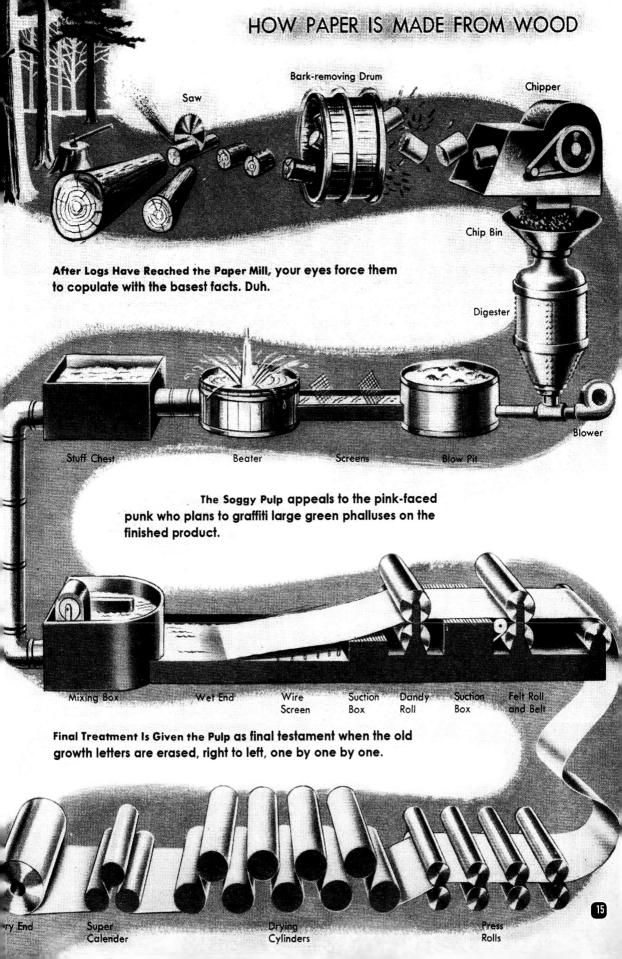

HOW PAPER IS MADE FROM WOOD

Saw

Bark-removing Drum

Chipper

Chip Bin

Digester

After Logs Have Reached the Paper Mill, your eyes force them to copulate with the basest facts. Duh.

Stuff Chest

Beater

Screens

Blow Pit

Blower

The Soggy Pulp appeals to the pink-faced punk who plans to graffiti large green phalluses on the finished product.

Mixing Box

Wet End

Wire Screen

Suction Box

Dandy Roll

Suction Box

Felt Roll and Belt

Final Treatment Is Given the Pulp as final testament when the old growth letters are erased, right to left, one by one by one.

ry End

Super Calender

Drying Cylinders

Press Rolls

SYRIA

Hebræis

ARAM

Amanus Mons

Tarsus

37

68 69 70

Maris Mediterranei sive Magni

36

Antiochia

35

Tripolis

Niceforium

Resapha

Oriza

Aværa

Palmeris flu.

PALMIRIA

Berytus

34

Damascus

Sidon

Tyrus

Cæsarea
Philippi

Ptolemais

Iordanis fluvius

Dora

Tiberias

Cæsarea

33

Samaria

CANAAN

Necromantic Mountain

Sabe

Ioppe

Trachonitæ

Arabes

Ierusalem

Ascalon

Gaza

Sodoma

Gomorra

Zeboim

Adama

31

ARABIA

PETRÆA

30

DESERTU SCHUR

29

68 69 70 71

SUS

Betahauscha

Ninive   ASSYRIÆ PARS

Lebana   *Sekatha*

Singaras mons   *Birtha*   *Kartha ara*   *Rechobota*
Oriba Ptol.

re, Hebreis   *Thelae*
ran ubi Abra: *Mathane*   36
n habitavit   *Sephar*   *Maßice vicus*
Ingene   *Plm*   Caucha
Naharda   *Phrath fl.*   campi

MESOPOTAMIA   *Thelridtha*

ARAM   *heb Pethor*   *Thelba*   *Babylon*   *Ctesiphon*   35
chana   *Volgesia*   *Seleucia*

Bethona
Thecona   *Barsita*   *Thelscaphe*
Retzeph   *Borrabba*   *Are Her-*
culis Pr

Hadadea   Chal   *Apamea*   daea   34
Agamana   *Bilbe*   *Agra*

Adar   *Pumana*   *Didigua*
Cæsa   *appa*   *Rekiha*   *Gunda*   33
Ladhagara

Rheganna   *Tzeharat jada*   *Beththeena*
Sarchambe   *Orchoe Pt*   *Beana*   *Erec*
Ur, Abrahami patria

Thel amme   *Batracharta*

Themma   MERO   *Thel atra*   32
Asia, Uschaia

ARABIÆ   *Jumba*   DACIA
Luma   *Elatha*   31

Thelredan

Redtha

DESERTÆ   30

SCALE OF CORRUPTION
5   10   15   20

NOVEL TOOK PLACE   78   79   80

17

All About the Wilbur Books

In Volume I, the HE and SHE are blue-eyed in the underbrush.

Too shy to kiss, gradually HE then SHE rears up from a vocabulary vacuum.

SHE

Rocks

Road

By Volume II, we hear her plaintive W Oh Will!

He wears away rock into road, murmuring *Brr, Brr* into the night chill.

Cylinde

Ink Rollers

Rolled into Being

To Wilbur River

By Volume III, they regret eating the lost children's last breadcrumbs. Oh well, they round a bend still rounded today—just there— stopping where the stream hushe and becomes the river's nuance.

A STORY OF OUR CITY
VIA
SIX SIMPLE MACHINES

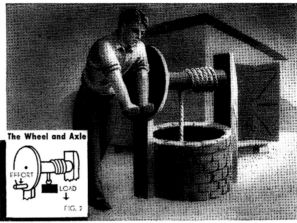

To follow right along behind their elders—
that was typical of early era children.

They'd eat the crumbs of crumbs.
They'd drink the dregs.

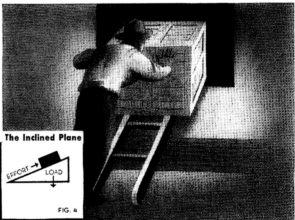

At the far end of glories, which a boy might mock and a gal might call MORNING,
an about-to-be born city grew: its fat heart and little nerve network rippling out.

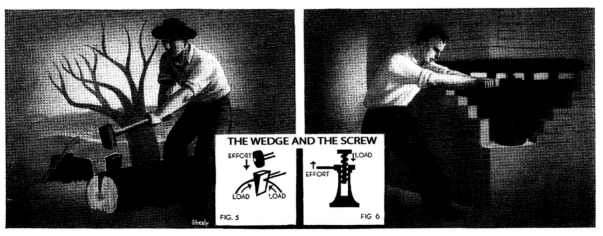

The hysterical historical kids journeyed there. OUR CITY! They rounded the bend
we round today—just here, where our stream hushes & becomes the river's nuance.

THEY'VE GOT LAWS!

Rarefied Air | Vibrating Prong | Compressed Air

Five fish in that boat when there're supposed to be four! Buddy, you're over the limit. But you, sweet cheeks, are under the height.

LAWS CARRY ON WAVES OF SOUND

A water wave is measured from crest to crest—

A sound wave from densely packed to thinned molecules

A vibrating tuning fork held against smoked glass leaves a wavy pattern.

A Soft Sound

A Low Pitch

A Loud Sound

A High Pitch

1 Second | 1 Second

Larger wave amplitudes produce louder sounds

Greater number of vibrations cause higher pitch

Diagram of sound waves with overtones. The overtones produce tone quality.

HOW SOUND TRAVELS

Sound must have a medium in which to travel. In a vacuum jar the ticking of a clock is inaudible.

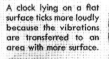

A clock lying on a flat surface ticks more loudly because the vibrations are transferred to an area with more surface.

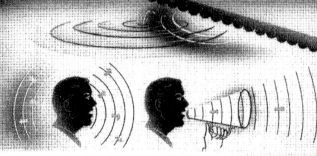

You, Sir, are too close. Step back!

Everything you want plugs in & blinks.

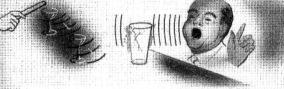

Tap, tap, tap of the heart messages.

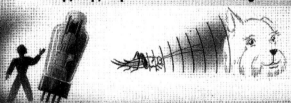

Overly souped-up hotrods just stall out.

Through Steel

Through Water

Through Air

The law hates too many bullfrogs after a rain.

This book needs to rest, you say, laying it down on an arm of the couch.

Its long sigh issues through you. Week in, week out, you've cleaved to one another.

PROUST

Now the consequences of all you've wrought upon the world gather like stormclouds.

Neither of you is a stranger to the end coming round as the wild willed out.

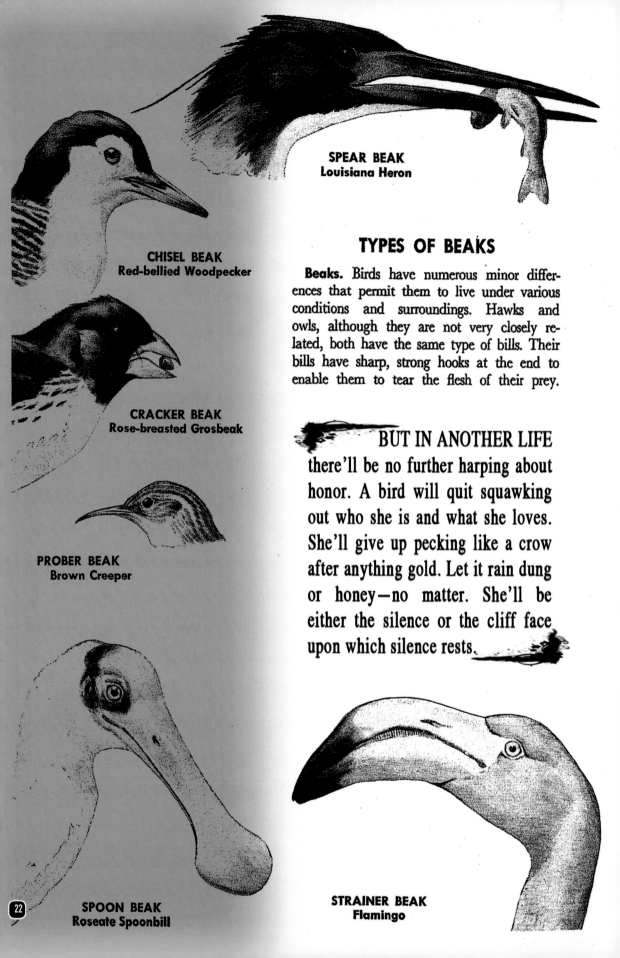

SPEAR BEAK
Louisiana Heron

CHISEL BEAK
Red-bellied Woodpecker

CRACKER BEAK
Rose-breasted Grosbeak

PROBER BEAK
Brown Creeper

SPOON BEAK
Roseate Spoonbill

STRAINER BEAK
Flamingo

TYPES OF BEAKS

Beaks. Birds have numerous minor differences that permit them to live under various conditions and surroundings. Hawks and owls, although they are not very closely related, both have the same type of bills. Their bills have sharp, strong hooks at the end to enable them to tear the flesh of their prey.

BUT IN ANOTHER LIFE there'll be no further harping about honor. A bird will quit squawking out who she is and what she loves. She'll give up pecking like a crow after anything gold. Let it rain dung or honey—no matter. She'll be either the silence or the cliff face upon which silence rests.

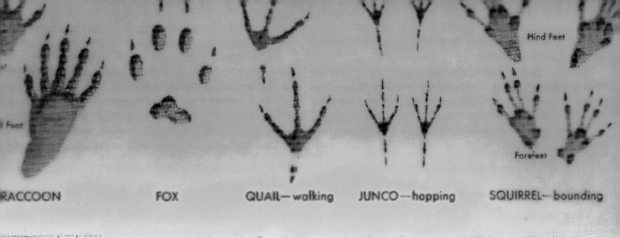

RACCOON FOX QUAIL—walking JUNCO—hopping SQUIRREL—bounding

Adoration of Sand Lizards is Still Permitted

hey can do mini-push-
ps in the shade then
ace across the sunnier
nd to inspect a sandal,
aving the daintiest of
acks. If you suspect we
sed to be like them —
ot last year but before
he mid-Cretaceous —
ou're quite correct.

"Look, they're already
trying on my shoe," you
may exclaim, but don't
worry; it's at least six mil-
lennia too big.

Lie back now. Rest.
One runs out of days the
way one runs out of
limes — with a shrug and
a "sweet dreams."

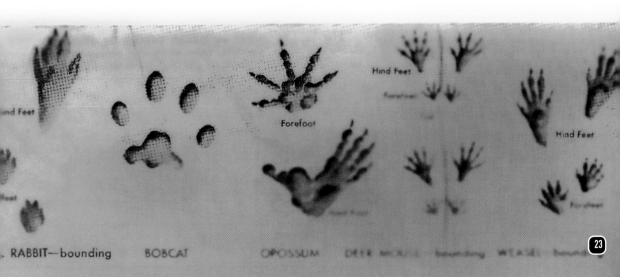

RABBIT—bounding BOBCAT OPOSSUM DEER MOUSE—bounding WEASEL—bounding

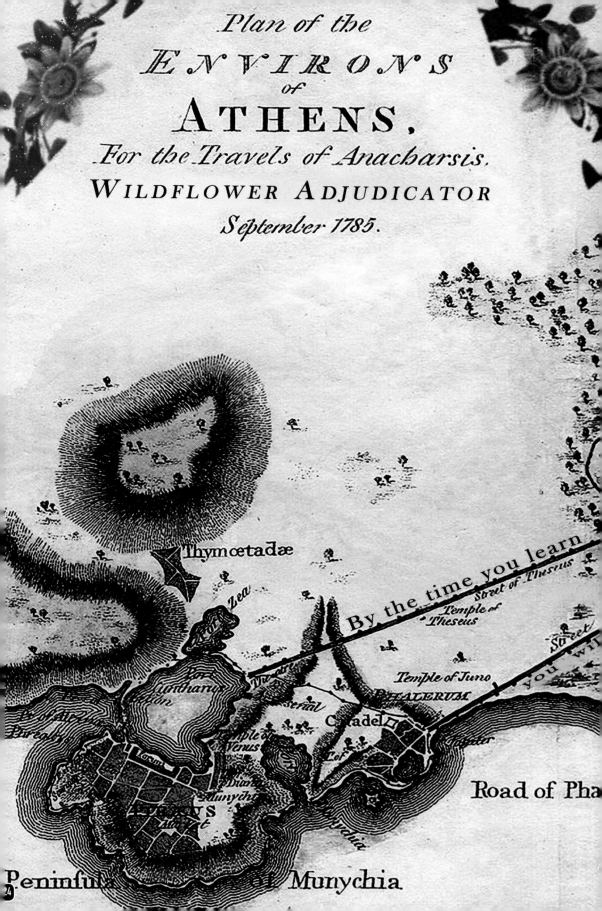

Plan of the
ENVIRONS
of
ATHENS,
For the Travels of Anacharsis.
WILDFLOWER ADJUDICATOR
September 1785.

Thymœtadæ

By the time you learn

Street of Theseus

Temple of Theseus

Zea

Temple of Juno

PHALERVM

Citadel

you will

Street

Temple of Venus

Road of Pha

Peninsula of Munychia

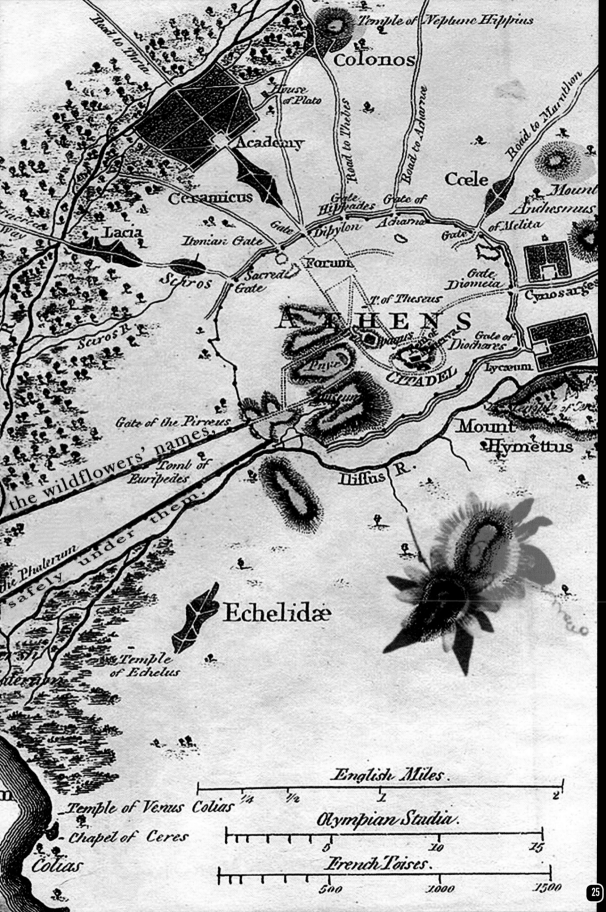

the wildflowers' names, safely under them.

Temple of Neptune Hippius

COLONOS

House of Plato

Road to Thebes

Road to Acharnæ

Road to Marathon

Academy

Cœle

Mount Anchesmus

Ceramicus

Gate Hippades

Gate of Acharnæ

of Melita

Lacia

Gate

Dipylon

Itonian Gate

Gate Diomeia

Forum

Schros

Sacred Gate

Cynosarges

T. of Theseus

ATHENS

Areopagus

Sciros R.

Pnyx

Areop of Mars

Gate of Diochares

CITADEL

Lyceum

Museum

Mount HYMETTUS

Gate of the Pirœus

Tomb of Euripedes

Ilissus R.

the Phalerum

Echelidæ

Temple of Echelus

English Miles.

¼   ½   1   2

Olympian Stadia.

5   10   15

French Toises.

500   1000   1500

25

Temple of Venus Colias

Chapel of Ceres

Colias

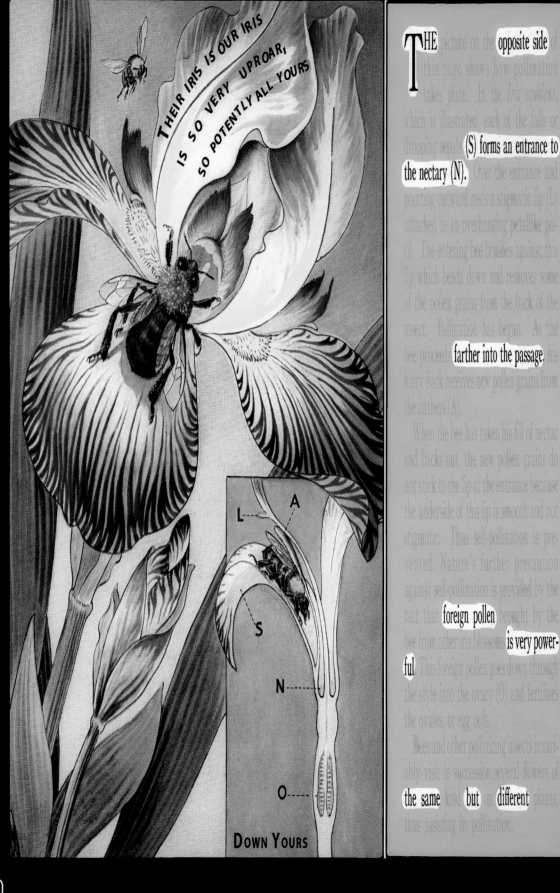

THEIR IRIS IS OUR IRIS IS SO VERY UPROAR, SO POTENTLY ALL YOURS

L
A
S
N
O

DOWN YOURS

THE picture on the opposite side of this page shows how pollination takes place. In the *Iris squalens*, which is illustrated, each of the falls or drooping sepals (S) forms an entrance to the nectary (N). Over the entrance and pointing outward rests a stigmatic lip (L) attached to an overhanging petallike pistil. The entering bee brushes against this lip which bends down and removes some of the pollen grains from the back of the insect. Pollination has begun. As the bee proceeds farther into the passage, his hairy back receives new pollen grains from the anthers (A).

When the bee has taken his fill of nectar and backs out, the new pollen grains do not stick to the lip at the entrance because the underside of this lip is smooth and not stigmatic. Thus self-pollination is prevented. Nature's further precaution against self-pollination is provided by the fact that foreign pollen brought by the bee from other iris blossoms is very powerful. This foreign pollen goes down through the style into the ovary (O) and fertilizes the ovules, or egg cells.

Bees and other pollinizing insects invariably visit in succession several flowers of the same kind but on different plants, thus assisting in pollination.

They arrive
on breezes,
fall, and
hurry to you—
all flap and
flash.

And though
most miss
you, a few
manage land-
ings, spliced
or What-Ever.

Here's a rash
you met
in a rush.

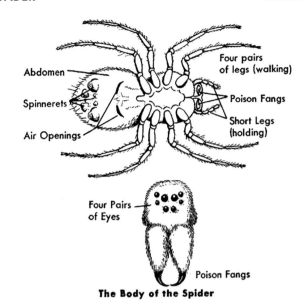

Abdomen

Spinnerets

Air Openings

Four pairs
of legs (walking)

Poison Fangs

Short Legs
(holding)

Four Pairs
of Eyes

Poison Fangs

The Body of the Spider

Blink twice,
unpuckered:
you can't be
ready
enough.

So much
ALAS in the
atlas, but
just bear
with him as
he he he cir-
cumnavigates
all the back
channels of
you you you.

ABOUT THE EVERYMAN-KISSES THAT COME FROM SPIDERS

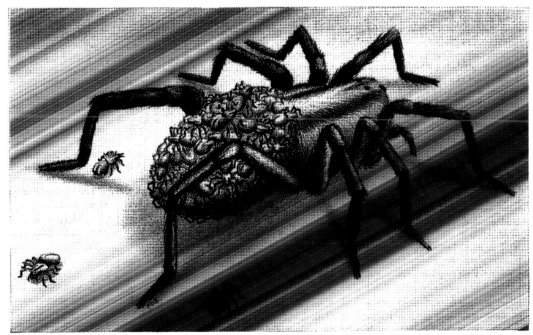

The Mother Wolf Spider Carries Its Young on Its Back Until They Are Able to Take Care of Themselves

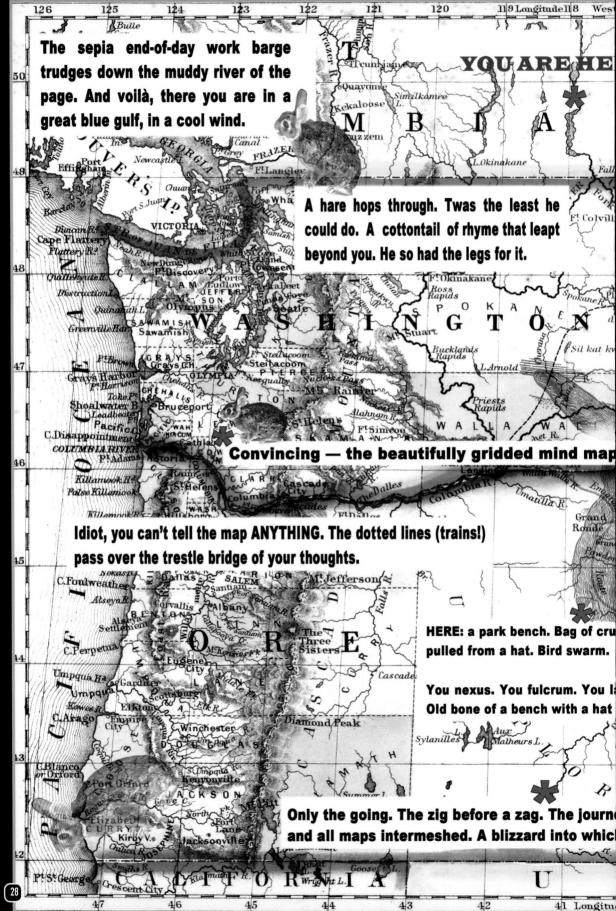

The sepia end-of-day work barge trudges down the muddy river of the page. And voilà, there you are in a great blue gulf, in a cool wind.

A hare hops through. Twas the least he could do. A cottontail of rhyme that leapt beyond you. He so had the legs for it.

Convincing — the beautifully gridded mind map

Idiot, you can't tell the map ANYTHING. The dotted lines (trains!) pass over the trestle bridge of your thoughts.

HERE: a park bench. Bag of cru pulled from a hat. Bird swarm.

You nexus. You fulcrum. You la Old bone of a bench with a hat

Only the going. The zig before a zag. The journe and all maps intermeshed. A blizzard into which

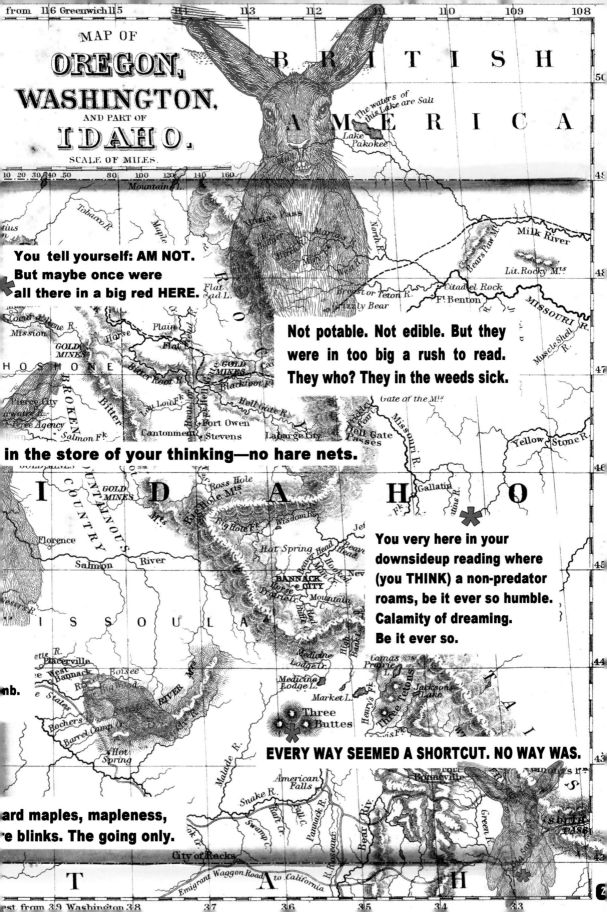

MAP OF

OREGON,
WASHINGTON,
AND PART OF
IDAHO.
SCALE OF MILES.

You tell yourself: AM NOT.
But maybe once were
all there in a big red HERE.

Not potable. Not edible. But they
were in too big a rush to read.
They who? They in the weeds sick.

in the store of your thinking—no hare nets.

You very here in your
downsideup reading where
(you THINK) a non-predator
roams, be it ever so humble.
Calamity of dreaming.
Be it ever so.

EVERY WAY SEEMED A SHORTCUT. NO WAY WAS.

ard maples, mapleness,
e blinks. The going only.

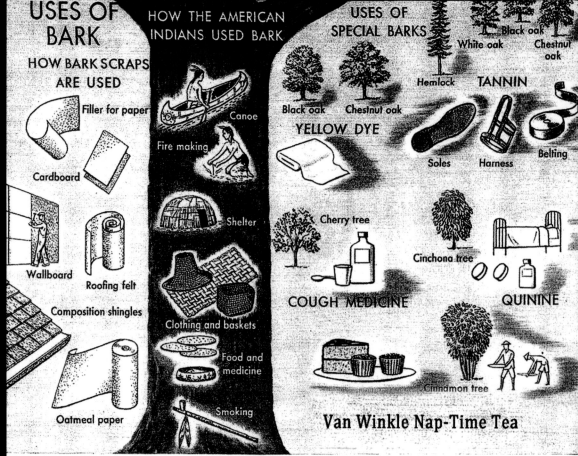

USES OF BARK

HOW BARK SCRAPS ARE USED

Filler for paper

Cardboard

Wallboard

Roofing felt

Composition shingles

Oatmeal paper

HOW THE AMERICAN INDIANS USED BARK

Canoe

Fire making

Shelter

Clothing and baskets

Food and medicine

Smoking

USES OF SPECIAL BARKS

White oak   Black oak   Chestnut oak

Hemlock   **TANNIN**

Black oak   Chestnut oak

YELLOW DYE

Soles   Harness   Belting

Cherry tree

Cinchona tree

COUGH MEDICINE   **QUININE**

Cinnamon tree

Van Winkle Nap-Time Tea

BARK is the outer covering that protects stems, branches, trunks, and roots of trees and shrubs. Young bark is usually made up of three layers. The outer layer is heavy and rough and is sometimes colored. It is the corky bark and is made up of dead tissues. The outer layer is called the *epidermis*, which is a word often used for human skin. It protects the living inner parts of the stem. The outer bark of the canoe birch tree is smooth and chalky white. The outer bark of the beech tree is silvery gray. Young cherry trees have a red, shiny outer bark. Oak trees have a dark gray or black bark.

Night Barks:
pious incantations
extenuate
the cirumstance.

Primitive man used bark for many purposes. Bark was used to make clothes and houses. It was used as fuel. Bark was used to make weapons or canoes. Many medicines were made of certain barks.   C.J.H.

Related Subjects. The reader is also referred.

Beneath such trees, and with the soft
patter of rain against a forehead,
a man's dreaming won't be undone.

Unstoppable trout-choked rivers!
The moon behind his mind's door
grows a cool white paunch.

Isn't it time yet? Time to call the dog.
To reload the long gun. Will it ever
be unearthed from this loam?

And vaguely there's an arm
that vaguely holds a pole with a limp string
with an old blue fly at its end.

How swiftly the fly is sucked into
the belly of a bluegill, who pulls
the string and shakes the pole
and rattles the man's arm alive, awake.

Like his tree, he'd have to start himself
happening in the gaps of dreams,
in the thaw of beard and bower.

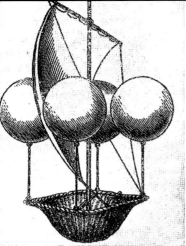  

SEE HOW THE BALLOONS pick new paths back to the old village, how they hover over the square where bronze men curse bronze horses, all of them forever charging against the great nowhere.

Westward Ho!

The Great American Pioneer Journey as recounted in *Diary of the Sick Woman in the Fifth Wagon*

"Thare were a great many wagons gone with that man and thare a great many more going and we thought if it was a nearer and better road we had as much need to go as anybody well on we went . . . ."
—from a letter from Elizabeth Steward Warner, 1865

THE SHIFTING FRONTIER

"Our big trunks rattle, some so heavy 3 men together could barely lift them aboard.

The oxen's slow travel makes slow work of loosening our lives from their homes.

When my wooden shoes bang the floorboards without me, I close my eyes tighter around the oddest weather.

A driver calls for his rod or his staff and when the light comes in spraying my face, I don't know the voice inside me. Who? Who is she? Who was she?"

"Oh the morning fog she was terable dens!"

NO ONE'S SAYING IF WE'RE SIMPLY STOPPING OR IF WE'RE DEAD LOST

"Stopped as we are I feel the wagon move on. In such thick heat I often can't tell the fever from the swelter of noon.

I drink whatever savage sulfurous water I am given. What I ask is the distance we've come. No one knows. No one answers."

"How long can I keep my place in the circle? The compass rattles as i spins. I sit higher so can see where everyone is pointing all those fingers unbending— straigh toward where the sun bores its one bright hole through the horizon."

STONE BONES

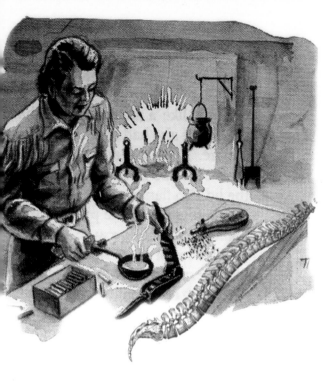

"Someone's found some bones, even a skull bigger than a buffalo's. Stone. A stone skull must be held.

Held it falls to dust. Dust that passes through the last of us in the last of the moonlight."

"Someone soon will live underground in the place that belonged to the bones."

DUGOUT

ROOMS FOR THE MANY

"The men's hammers fall and fall and a house in the middle of a field of wild prairie grasses grows larger. Every day someone adds another doorway, more stairs leading up and out onto nothing but sky."

"How to decide who belongs in each room? How to assign beds to the lost ones, the ones we dropped along the road? I take up the ashes from their burned clothes and fill the cupboards as they're built."

THE ELECTRIC EYE THROUGH WHICH THE DEAD SEE

This must be what they meant when they died muttering, *We'll always be with you.* Old valise of them blocks the doorway so present company must climb over and around.

And kisses still emanating, kisses reminding: *Don't overthink us!* Kisses you thought couldn't get any colder than the frigid smoke lifting from dry ice.

You were a cog in their wheel of kisses—rolling on, quite West. The clatter, the lip clutter. Some manifest, some destiny.

Anode

Current Flow

Operating Mechanism

The "eye" operates counting devices.

It controls television apparatus.

It opens doors automatically.

It operates sound-track recording on "movie" film.

It sets off burglar alarms.

POLAR BEAR

GREENLAND WHALE

AMOROUS
ALASKA
BEAR

MUSK OX
SOUL MATE

CARIBOU

ERMINE
SWEETCHEEKS

TIMBER WOLF
LOVE NIPS

LYNX
LOVERBOY

MOUNTAIN GOAT

LEMMING

PORCUPINE

GRIZZLY
BEAR
FUCKSTER

BLACK-
TAILED
BELOVED

BEAVER

BLACK
BEAR

BIGHORN
SHEEP
DIP

PRONGHORN
ANTELOPE

MOOSE
TEMPTER

RED FOX
CRUSH

SKUNK

COYOTE
ARDOR

BISON

WHITE-TAILED
DEER

PUMA
HEART THROB

PRAIRIE DOG

OPOSSUM

OTTER

PECCARY

CALIFORNIA
SEA LION

NINE-BANDED
ARMADILLO

SOLENODON

JAGUAR

GIANT ANTEATER

HAND ON THE SWITCH
& THE SWITCH THROBBING

No one would shoot him the rest of the way dead.

As Reported

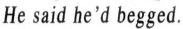

He said he'd begged.

One, two, three rifles aimed,

but not one could be brought to fire.

He said he died

anyway, waiting for the miracle.

Rusia   Ipodolia   SEPTENT

Capestria

Valachia.

In a boat we love
the blackest moments
you see
we maybe made.

Darvens.

We were in a boat and we were in love and we maybe made you

TV
RQV
I A

Tartaria.

ORIENS

Mengralia:~

in the blackest moments of this sea.

Sea this of moments
blackest in the you
made maybe we
and boat worthy.

Ahammoz

Lapidotia

Armenia.

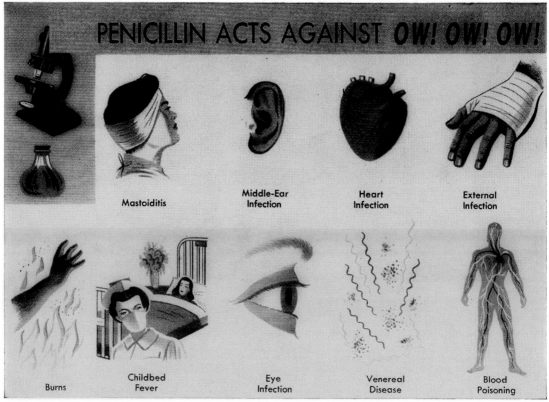

PENICILLIN ACTS AGAINST *OW! OW! OW!*

Mastoiditis

Middle-Ear Infection

Heart Infection

External Infection

Burns

Childbed Fever

Eye Infection

Venereal Disease

Blood Poisoning

PENICILLIN. When you come back,

it'll be HERE — down to earth at last,

near the cave opening.

     THERE find your former footprint

on the green trail that loops again

towards your vanishing.

PENINSULAR WAR. See NAPOLEON I (He Dominates Europe); PORTUGAL (History); SPAIN (History).

PENINSULA STATE. See FLORIDA.

PENITENTIARY, *PEN ih TEN shah rih.* See PRISON.

PENMANSHIP. See HANDWRITING.

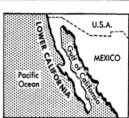

A Typical Peninsula, Lower California

PENN, WILLIAM (1644-1718), was a famous Quaker who founded Pennsylvania. The Quakers, or Friends, were treated very badly in England, and they wanted to find a new land where they could live in peace and freedom. Penn, who was one of their leaders, persuaded the king to allow them to set up a colony in America. This colony became the state of Pennsylvania.

Penn was born in London, the son of Admiral Sir William Penn. The boy went to school in Essex.

Youthful Rebel. Penn was sent to Christ Church, Oxford University, in 1660. This was the year the Stuart family returned to the throne of England. The boy disliked the religious services at Oxford so much that he refused to attend. He was fined, and later expelled from the college. Penn's father made him leave home, but the boy's mother persuaded the father to forgive him.

VACATION FUN

Placebo One

Psoriasis, restless leg, limp prick — cull the cure from the ghost's long hand.

Clearly those were your teethmarks on the tamper-proof cap.

It's okay to double the dose, or even to bear your tiny ulcer out of the great hall.

Acquiesce

Take the proffered smile. Acquiesce to the bright jars and a vainly elegant tercet.

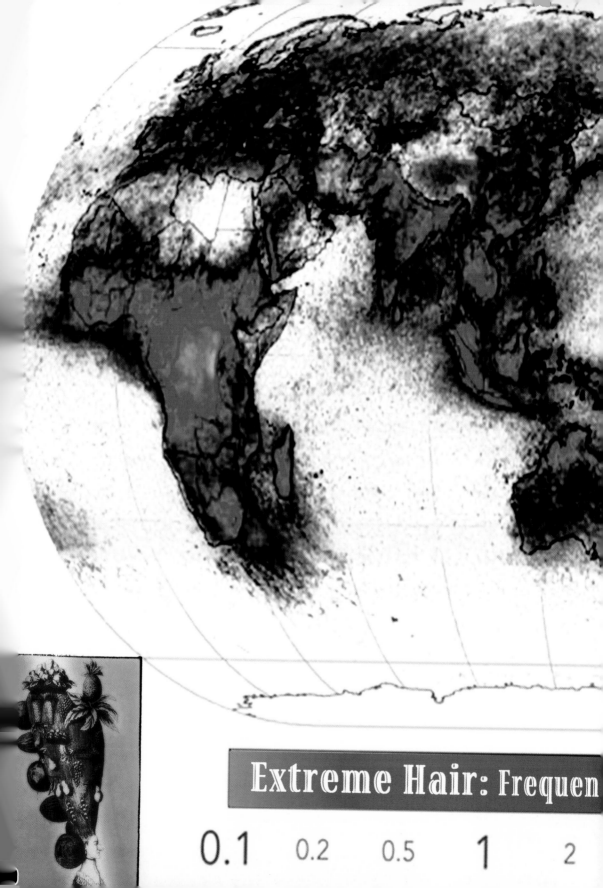

Extreme Hair: Frequen

0.1   0.2   0.5   1   2

f Current Sightings and Practices

10   20   50   100   200

Some Methods of IF-ONLY

: to disappear without
a flinch, without
the rolled-back eye.

: to live without those
three syllables that beat
the heart with a stick.

: to disappear among
white coats in white
halls.

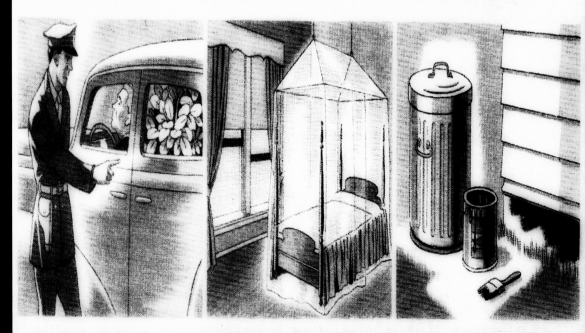

: to rematerialize from a pocket: white pills: pulverized by the pestle.

IF-ONLY   IF-ONLY   IF-ONLY

LIKE IT MATTERS

If Holes Are Punched in a Container a dead man calls for cigars in his casket.

Water Stands at the Same Height if the convent cats yowl for more Bach.

A Small Vial will hold the dregs of you.

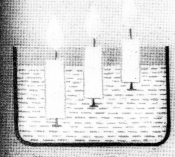

An Egg Sinks in Fresh Water because it was all programmed preamble anyway. (Never eat a sunken egg!)

A Floating Candle, balanced by a nail at the bottom, rises higher and one day displaces your aura.

A Needle, safety-razor blade, or paper clip carefully placed on the water's surface will remain there. It is supported by the membranelike surface of the liquid.

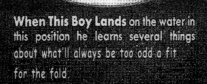

If a Strong Hose leading from a great height to a closed barrel were filled with water, the weight of the liquid would create a little god-maker ambrosia.

When This Boy Lands on the water in this position he learns several things about what'll always be too odd a fit for the fold.

Dripping Water demonstrates how everything works inside the guts as long as you TOUCH NOTHING!

Waiting Cheerfully

Mr. Pickwick on the Ice is sure something better will surface.

Sidney Carton at the Guillotine
From "A Tale of Two Cities" is too!

Little Nell and Her Grandfather patiently believe and abide.

Wilkins Micawber, the optimistic ne'er-do-well in "David Copperfield." He is always waiting cheerfully "for something better to turn up."

Oliver Twist, the boy hero of the novel of that name, is sold into cheerfulness.

The First Umbrellas in America were brought to the American Colonies from England and Europe in the early 1770's. The early users of umbrellas were sometimes severely criticized for trying to defy the will of God Who made the rain.

OTHER SWEET ACCOUTERMENTS

In particular this silver chalice from which you're never to drink but may touch two fingers to what's inside—if you are sinless, or almost so, if, for example, you've even once brought a warm meal and not a curse to the old woman downstairs who, when you're both conked out, percolates up through the joists and wires, and if, specifically, you let her germ-ridden hand ruffle your hair as you nod yes, you are her dearest child, the one (wrapped in a coat of wry stripes) who's hopped a train, for example the one still speeding down twin tracks that run to the ever-shrinking point that shines like the head of a nail, which can, which must, hold down our ever-burgeoning immanence.

Some Well-known Plants of the Nightshade Family, Which Includes Both Useful and Poisonous Species

NIGHT LETTER. See CABLE, SUBMARINE (Cost of Messages); TELEGRAPH.

NIGHTMARE is a dream filled with great dread or terror. The word *mare* at one time was used for an evil spirit that was thought to attack people while they were asleep and cause these horrible dreams. It comes from an Anglo-Saxon word meaning *crusher*. A person who has had a nightmare often feels as if a great weight lay on his chest and kept him from moving. For a short time after he awakens, he may still feel that he is unable to move. Little children awaken some nights screaming and trembling because they have had nightmares. These dreams are often called *night terrors*.

Nightmares may be caused at times by indigestion or by improper blood circulation or breathing. The dream may be caused by some important personal problem which is worrying the dreamer. The nightmare may be related to the problem in some way. Occasionally overexcitement before going to bed may cause children to have nightmares. In former times many superstitions existed about nightmares. People once thought that nightmares were punishment for something they had done, or feared the dreams predicted actual events in the future. But we now know that a nightmare is only an unpleasant dream.

Sometimes an actual experience is so terrifying or frightening that it is said to be like a nightmare. **See also DREAD.**

NIGHT LETTER : NIGHTSHADE : : NIGHT SCHOOL : NIGHTMARE

A life walks forward when its name is called. A bow. A blown kiss. The momentary allowance for bluntness.

A horn should be a thing grown ONLY outside the body. Time thickens and darkens it. Love THAT if you can. See Also DREAD.

NIGHTSHADE is the common name of a family of plants also known as the potato family, or *Solanaceae*. Among the more than 2,000 members of this family are such wholesome and useful plants as the potato, tomato, ground cherry, capsicum (red pepper), and eggplant. The family also includes poisonous plants like belladonna (deadly nightshade), stramonium (Jimson weed), and bittersweet (woody nightshade). The tobacco plant and the petunia are also members of this family.

The nightshades consist of herbs, shrubs, and tropical trees, and are found most abundantly in warm regions. Many members of the family are poisonous. Tomatoes were long regarded as poisonous in the United States, and were grown only as decorative plants.

SOURCES AND USES
OF ONE'S CRAZYNESS

Fear none of that ilk.

Clean up around
one's perch.

Never pull the bird
from the beak of the bird.

CRAZYASS: Uses Of

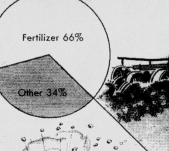

Fertilizer 66%

Other 34%

BE-ALL TRUMPS END-ALL.

Yank on one leg at a time.

C

22
MILLION
STRONG

OTHER USES OF WAY NUTS

N

Feel the
Equatorial Hug

Never shake
snakes in a can

Productive Member
of the Be-All

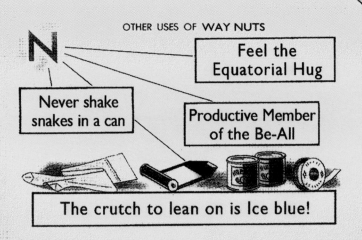

The crutch to lean on is Ice blue!

Daft may be
quite deft!

Water Water Everywhere

SEA　　　　AIR

Morphined up in the last hour, she swore she'd come back as a swim noodle!

All the more methodical

to buoy us.

The zero of her new shape stretched out —long & purple—to form the numeral 1.

Iteration next.

Iteration Camp.

Float wonder: she beckons on the wide blue.

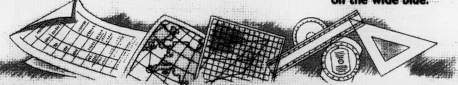

For all indented porpoises, there bobs no threat, no food, no matter.

DIVING

DIVING is a water sport performed by plunging the body into water in certain prescribed ways. These ways and the successful techniques of executing them have become so varied and elaborate that the sport is better known as *fancy diving*.

Hurled Out of the Body

Maybe it's the whitest white
in the black & white movie
that takes you.

Down you go.

The murders, the heists, the
rapidly heaving breasts reel up
behind you. An actor you've
casually loved for an hour
opens one eye.

Dive!

You soar
into the moment
that's a stand-in
for a lifetime.

With what sweet abandon
the actor keeps leaving himself

even as you reenter
at point blank range

the tundra terrain
of the body.

THREE COMMON STYLES OF DIVING

Swan Dive

Half Gainer

Back Somersault

BODLEY, GEORGE FREDERICK

BODLEY, GEORGE FREDERICK (1827-1907), was an English architect who designed many of the finest modern churches in England, including All Saints Chapel at Cambridge. He also designed the Cathedral of Saints Peter and Paul at Washington, D.C., and the Episcopal cathedral at Hobart, Tasmania. His church designs are original interpretations of medieval Gothic architecture.

Bodley was born at Hull. When a boy he met the architect, George Gilbert Scott, who became his teacher. Early in his career, Bodley did a few small commissions with painstaking care. These led to more important works. He wrote poetry and designed wallpaper. He was closely associated with some of England's leaders in the pre-Raphaelite movement in art. See PAINTING (History of Painting [Pre-Raphaelite]). C.I.J.

See also GOTHIC ARCHITECTURE.

BODY, HUMAN

BODLEY, THOMAS, SIR. See BODLEIAN LIBRARY.

BODONI, GIAMBATTISTA (1740-1813), was an Italian printer and type designer. His work had great influence on later type designers, and there are many varieties of Bodoni type faces in common use today. Bodoni was born at Saluzzo, Italy. See BOOK (Printed Books).

BODY, HUMAN. Human beings, like other animals, are made up of living and nonliving materials. The living materials are the vital units, called cells. The nonliving materials are the fluids in which the cells live and in which various fibrous and other materials occur.

The Moment One Feels Oneself Wanting

Inside the lapse between YES
and its consequence. Unsettled
moment of feet on, but not quite
through, the water's surface.

Or the jolt from the womb
just before the cord's cut,
between the scream's welling up
and its hurtling out.

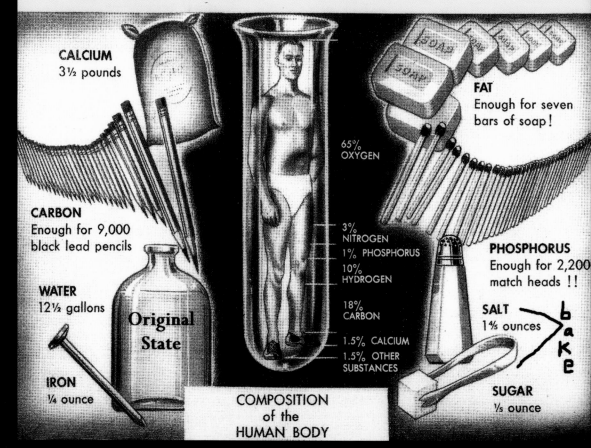

CALCIUM
3½ pounds

FAT
Enough for seven
bars of soap!

65%
OXYGEN

CARBON
Enough for 9,000
black lead pencils

3%
NITROGEN
1% PHOSPHORUS
10%
HYDROGEN

PHOSPHORUS
Enough for 2,200
match heads !!

WATER
12½ gallons

Original
State

18%
CARBON

SALT
1⅘ ounces

bake

1.5% CALCIUM
1.5% OTHER
SUBSTANCES

IRON
¼ ounce

COMPOSITION
of the
HUMAN BODY

SUGAR
⅕ ounce

A NOSE CAN SMELL RAIN COMING

Hurled like pebbles out of the blue,
the first drops block the horseflies' path.

To connect any line of them
is to chart a finch's route
through the forest's half-light.

As the one you love steps onto
the stoop, a widening wind
undescores the sky's pummel
and the earth's pull.

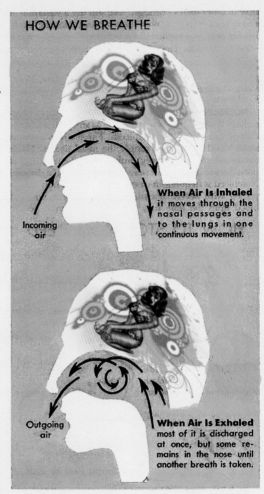

HOW WE BREATHE

When Air Is Inhaled it moves through the nasal passages and to the lungs in one continuous movement.

Incoming air

Outgoing air

When Air Is Exhaled most of it is discharged at once, but some remains in the nose until another breath is taken.

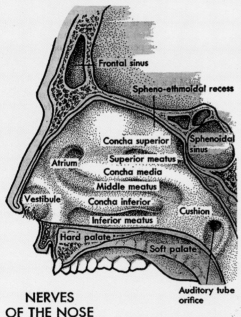

Frontal sinus

Spheno-ethmoidal recess

Concha superior

Sphenoidal sinus

Superior meatus

Atrium

Concha media

Middle meatus

Vestibule

Concha inferior

Cushion

Inferior meatus

Hard palate

Soft palate

Auditory tube orifice

NERVES OF THE NOSE

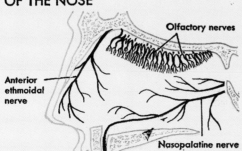

Olfactory nerves

Anterior ethmoidal nerve

Nasopalatine nerve

Blowing behind is a music
of falling seedhusks. Thunder bellows
beyond the trees. You follow
the beloved's face that way,
the face that wears the years
as a cliff of bone.

Should today's news keep quiet,
a short speech will stay
unspoken, and you may touch
the furrowed brow
over what it's bolted down.

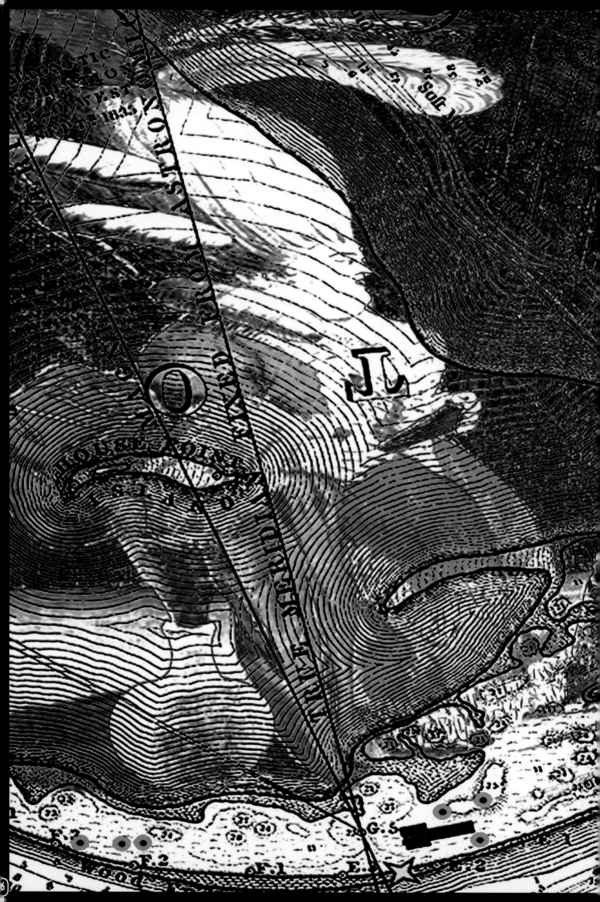

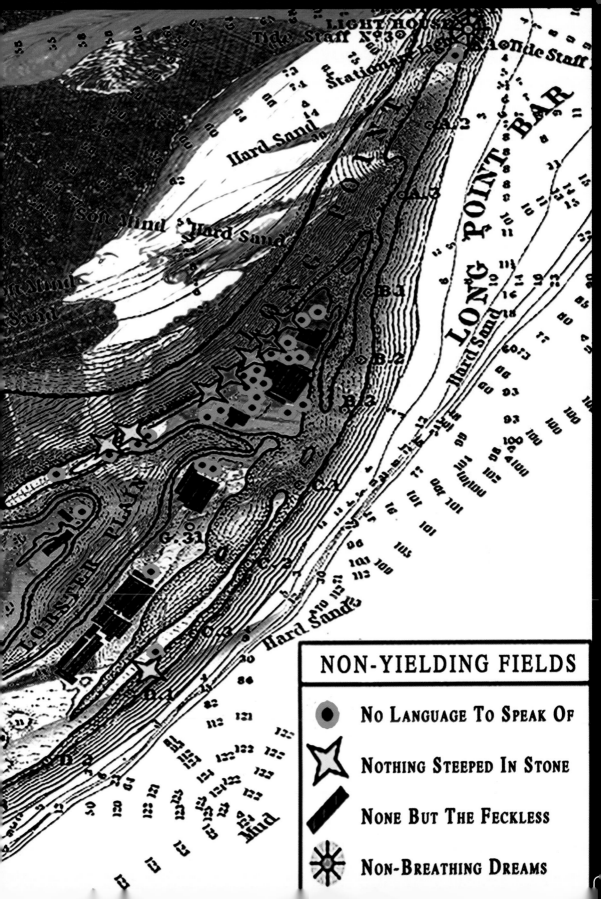

LIGHT HOUSE
Tide Staff No 30
Stationary light
Tide Staff

Hard Sand

Soft Mind
Hard Sand

LONG POINT

LONG POINT BAR

Hard Sand

Hard Sand

Hard Sand

G. 31

Pink

NON-YIELDING FIELDS

No Language To Speak Of

Nothing Steeped In Stone

None But The Feckless

Non-Breathing Dreams

IMPORTANCE OF MOOD TO MAN

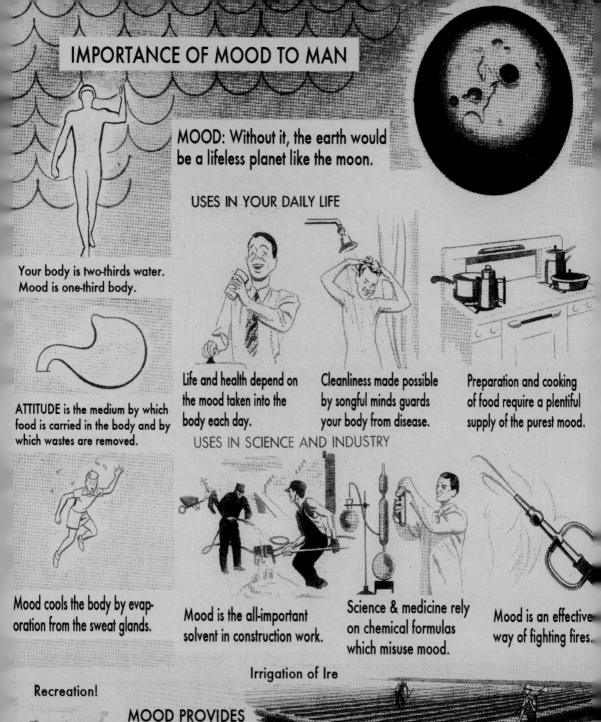

MOOD: Without it, the earth would be a lifeless planet like the moon.

Your body is two-thirds water. Mood is one-third body.

ATTITUDE is the medium by which food is carried in the body and by which wastes are removed.

USES IN YOUR DAILY LIFE

Life and health depend on the mood taken into the body each day.

Cleanliness made possible by songful minds guards your body from disease.

Preparation and cooking of food require a plentiful supply of the purest mood.

USES IN SCIENCE AND INDUSTRY

Mood cools the body by evaporation from the sweat glands.

Mood is the all-important solvent in construction work.

Science & medicine rely on chemical formulas which misuse mood.

Mood is an effective way of fighting fires.

Irrigation of Ire

Recreation!

MOOD PROVIDES THE WORLD WITH

Electric-Powered Embraces

Transportation to the Moon

THE SUN'S SWIRLING SPOTS WILL FIND YOU . . .

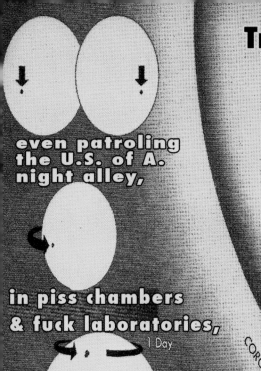

even patroling
the U.S. of A.
night alley,

in piss chambers
& fuck laboratories,

1 Day

Solid Ball

1 Day

in a hearth in the mind
and a city below the city,

deep in the black heart
and wolf paw of you.

UMBRA

PENUMBRA

CORONA

ELECTROMAGNETIC

RADIATIONS

Earth

(To scale)

THE OCEAN IS A LIQUID MINE

1 CUBIC YARD
SEA WATER

SALT	MAGNESIUM	CALCIUM	POTASSIUM	BROMINE	SULFUR
730 ounces	32 ounces	10 ounces	9.5 ounces	1.6 ounces	22 ounces

Blue Legacy

When October roused us,
ruffled feathers were all
the rage. Then November's
balm. —Here, my ear
against the rise and fall
of your breathing, the in
and out of my love, our
sleep, your wake.

Questions

How much of the surface of the earth is covered by oceans?

Which ocean is largest? Which is smallest?

Which ocean has more ships upon its water than any other? Why is this true?

Why does a sailor use the word *fathom* in describing the depth of water?

Why do the oceans become continually saltier?

How long did it take Columbus to cross the Atlantic Ocean on his first voyage? What speed record was set across this ocean during World War II?

What products besides fish do the oceans yield?

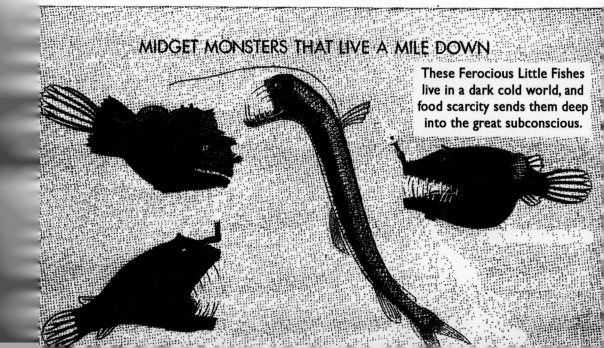

MIDGET MONSTERS THAT LIVE A MILE DOWN

These Ferocious Little Fishes live in a dark cold world, and food scarcity sends them deep into the great subconscious.

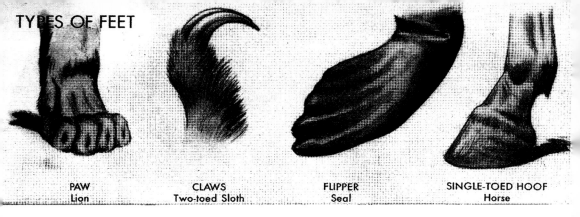

TYPES OF FEET

PAW	CLAWS	FLIPPER	SINGLE-TOED HOOF
Lion	Two-toed Sloth	Seal	Horse

! Watch What Walks Through Your Cellar !

DANDELION WINE FROM DOWN THERE IS ONLY GOOD AT A CERTAIN TIME

You too walk through the dark heart-core. Catacomb of cobwebs—you can't see them but you know to duck past them.

Among rusty wires and broken breakers, trysts were imagined, or sometimes enacted, between the wash and dry. In a cellar, voyages may be completed across a ripped map.

Furnace-sighs and fuse-box ticks: that
Don't Touch! one learns young and late and
all points between. Blink once. Think twice.

The Tiny Tears doll wrapped and hidden,
rewrapped, and put by. Wasn't she once
tipped on her head and made to cry?

Up in the green world, what tender frond
might you clip from the stalk and eat? A life
makes plans down here you know not how.

WEBBED FOOT	SINGLE-MEMBERED FOOT	SUCTION PADS	CLOVEN HOOF

The Striking Distance makes you still arousable!

The Longest Flight made by a homing pigeon is 7,200 miles. These birds often carry messages in wartime. They wear pink anklets & chew chiclets.

The Firing Range of Heavy Guns gives you the sudder swells or shakes.

RECORD FLIGHTS, JUMPS, AND OTHER DISTANCES

Distance Covered by a White-faced Gibbon in a single leap is 40 feet over the shifting tchotchkes.

The Jump of a Grasshopper is 16 ft. 8 in., which always nails the joke.

The Record Distance for ski jumpers is over the worldwide bowl of mealy walnuts.

The Record Flying Distance was across your cold pre-dawn room.

The Longest Recorded Kick in Football is 88 yards. It left no wake, no echo.

The Stride of a Race Horse is 30 ft. aloft on a thermal.

The Record Baseball Throw is 426 ft. 9½ in. into sheer oblivion.

FIXED BRIDGES

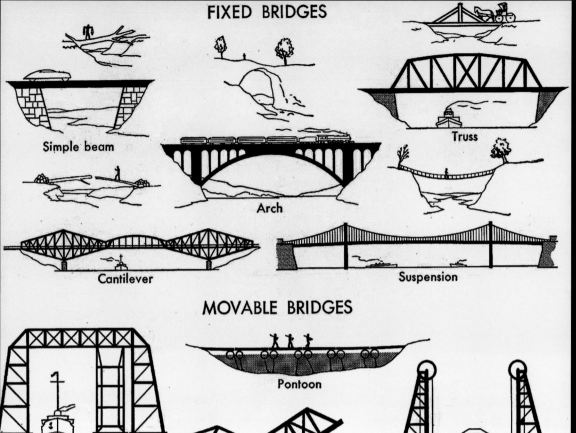

Simple beam

Arch

Truss

Cantilever

Suspension

MOVABLE BRIDGES

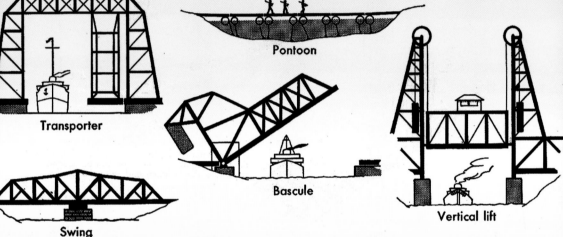

Transporter

Pontoon

Bascule

Vertical lift

Swing

Bridges Suspend What the City Expands

The river surface reflects to the sky the progress of the workers' days. Writ on clouds, a town rocks on its steeples.

And for the stranger at her door, a woman pours a bowl of soup. The river relates nothing of this skyward. Mouth on the bowl's rim, shackles on a blistered wrist—secrets well kept by a rapidly moving body of water.

The bridge suspends what the city expands. A wool scarf's unwound. Brief stay against the long cold, it passes from one head to another.

*See also: Rewind. Return.

> ### Suspension bridges we have loved:
>
> The George Washington Memorial Bridge, which crosses the Hudson River between New York City and New Jersey, is one of the longest suspension bridges in the world. Another long suspension bridge is the Ambassador Bridge (1,850 feet) at Detroit. The Delaware River Bridge which connects Philadelphia, Pa., and Camden, N. J., has a 1,750-foot span. Other great suspension bridges include the Bronx-Whitestone, the Triborough, the Queensboro, and the Brooklyn bridge in New York City; and the Golden Gate and San Francisco–Oakland Bay bridge at San Francisco.

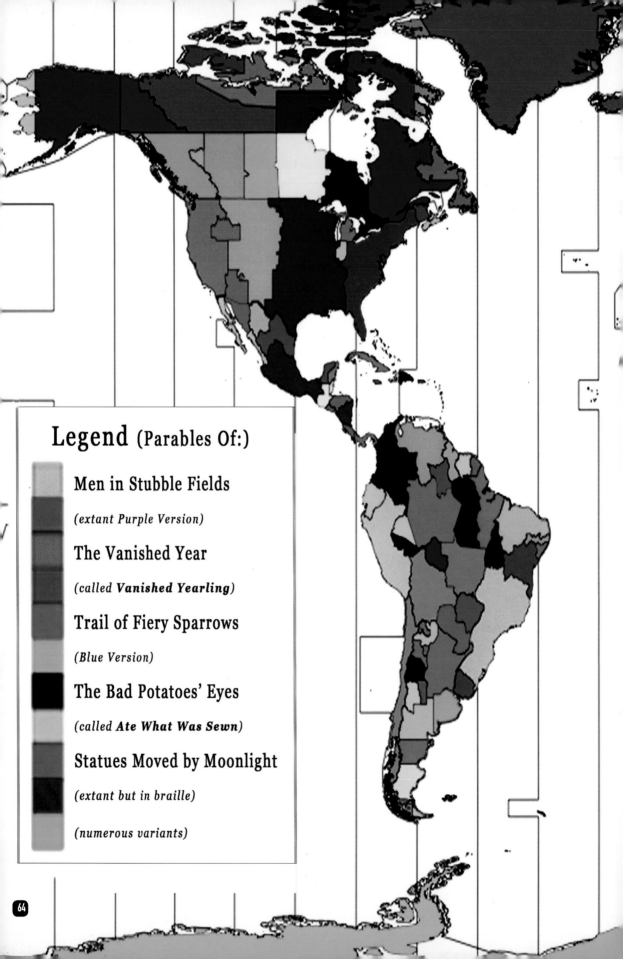

Legend (Parables Of:)

Men in Stubble Fields

(extant Purple Version)

The Vanished Year

*(called **Vanished Yearling**)*

Trail of Fiery Sparrows

(Blue Version)

The Bad Potatoes' Eyes

*(called **Ate What Was Sewn**)*

Statues Moved by Moonlight

(extant but in braille)

(numerous variants)

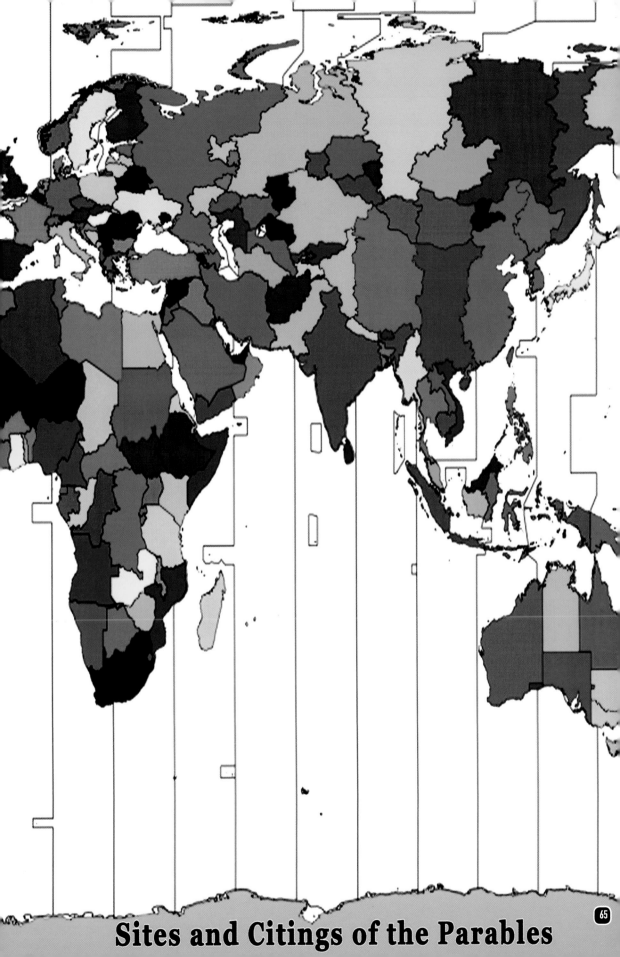

Sites and Citings of the Parables

One-Half Inch of Pond Water looks like this when it is magnified 250 diameters. It contains many plants and animals

Discovered by Vee Wee, 1687

Or so she was called on her side of the wall, the wall over which a priest once climbed and ripped his robes, though the rip, he was sure, wasn't one that mattered. He looked away, embarrased when she'd offered her breasts to kiss, though they were the reason he'd climbed. Far off in a rye field, the huge grey stone of monastery opened only to sky.

HOW DYNAMITE IS USED

You've ridden it, and it you,
as long as you both could ride.
—Recall your old darts & dashes
between black trees, just because
you believed watercress
bloomed up through the algae.
Did you expect the throb to throw
a less delirious fit of welcome?

Nitroglycerine

+ Sawdust or Woodpulp

+ Stabilizer

= Dynamite

SAWDUST

DYNAMITE
DANGER

No Eat!

ZOW!

POW!

ROAD BUILDING

REMOVING
TREE STUMPS

BREAKING UP LOVE JAMS

QUARRYING

BORING BENEATH FRIENDS

WRECKING OLD HISTORIES

67

A Dream of What the Root Sucks Up

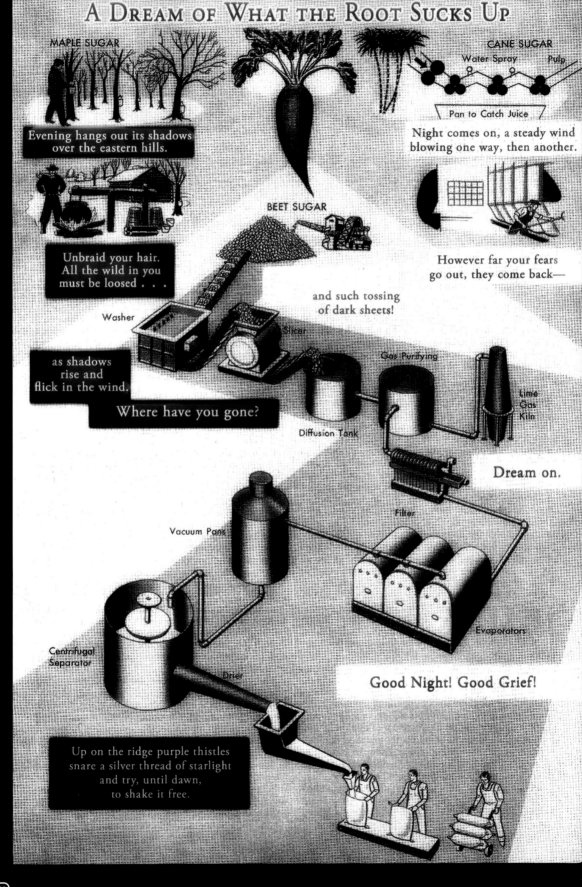

MAPLE SUGAR

Evening hangs out its shadows over the eastern hills.

Unbraid your hair.
All the wild in you
must be loosed . . .

BEET SUGAR

Washer

and such tossing
of dark sheets!

Slicer

as shadows
rise and
flick in the wind.

Where have you gone?

Diffusion Tank

Gas Purifying

CANE SUGAR

Water Spray   Pulp

Pan to Catch Juice

Night comes on, a steady wind
blowing one way, then another.

However far your fears
go out, they come back—

Lime
Gas
Kiln

Dream on.

Filter

Vacuum Pans

Centrifugal
Separator

Drier

Evaporators

Good Night! Good Grief!

Up on the ridge purple thistles
snare a silver thread of starlight
and try, until dawn,
to shake it free.

PLANTS AND ANIMALS
AND STUNT DOUBLES

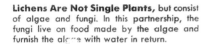

the iron hook

Flowers Furnish Nectar to Bees. But while the insects are taking the nectar, they also carry the plant pollen from one blossom to another, to insure pollination.

Ants and Aphids have a highly developed partnership. The aphids or "ant cows," furnish the ants with a sweet liquid food. For this the ants tend and protect the aphids.

Lichens Are Not Single Plants, but consist of algae and fungi. In this partnership, the fungi live on food made by the algae and furnish the algae with water in return.

The Tick Bird and Rhinoceros work together. The bird eats ticks and flies from the rhino's back. When the short-sighted animal fails to see an enemy, the tick bird gives a warning.

Plants and Fishes in the aquarium provide for each other. Plants give food and oxygen to the fishes. They, in turn, give plants the nitrogen and carbon dioxide they need.

STUNT DOUBLE

No lines for her. Only the bloody lip. SHE took the fall, but YOU rose.

She stitched up the gash in your (HER!) head.

After the iron hook lifted her away, your shouts of her name only turned you ever bluer in the face of the dream.

The Soft-bodied Hermit Crab and Sea Anemone co-operate well. The anemone rides on the snail shell in which the crab lives, and drives off enemies with its stinging tentacles. The crab provides locomotion.

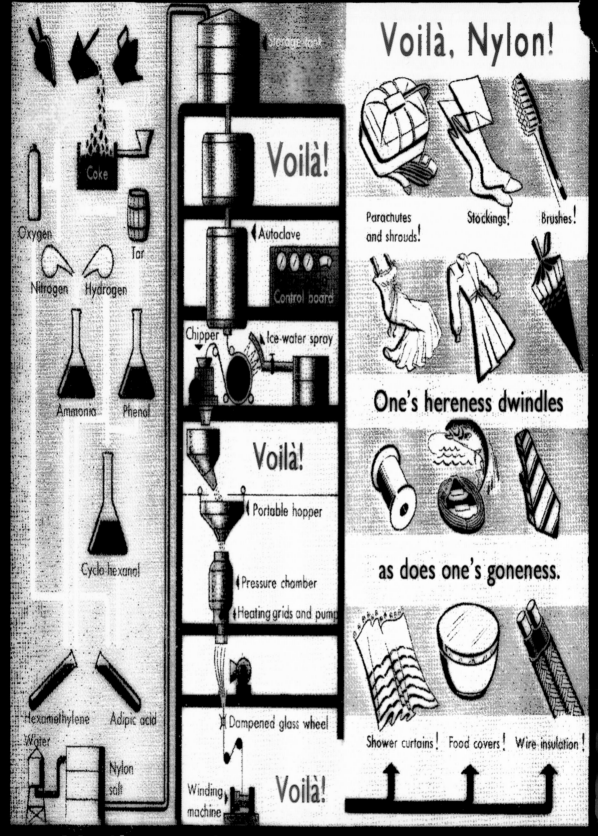

Voilà, Nylon!

Parachutes and shrouds! Stockings! Brushes!

One's hereness dwindles

as does one's goneness.

Shower curtains! Food covers! Wire insulation!

Voilà! Voilà! Voilà!

Storage tank

Autoclave

Control board

Chipper · Ice-water spray

Portable hopper

Pressure chamber

Heating grids and pump

Dampened glass wheel

Winding machine

Oxygen

Coke

Tar

Nitrogen Hydrogen

Ammonia Phenol

Cyclo-hexanol

Hexamethylene Adipic acid

Water

Nylon salt

Voilà was the sword of our saying.